Paul William Johnson

Daily and Monthly Inspirational Thoughts for a Year

ISBN 978-1-66788-866-8 eBook 978-1-66788-867-5

CONTENTS

INTRODUCTION

The following daily and monthly thoughts are based on my personal experience and are shared with you to help make your day more interesting, to provide you with daily and monthly inspiration and to help make your life more exciting and enjoyable.

Since I came into this magnificent world in 1940, I have had a never-ending curiosity about how things work. I have spent a lifetime exploring and working in public and private organizations and in owning and operating several professional and private businesses. In addition, I have participated in musical, religious and metaphysical organizations. The daily and monthly thoughts in this book originated from my personal notes, collected over the years, to help me better understand my daily experiences. The thoughts in this book are also written to help you understand how our physical or outer world works in conjunction our spiritual or inner world.

An expanded discussion of some of these thoughts can be found in my previous books.

This book contains a variety of subjects that I would like to share with you. It is intended only for your enjoyment and to possibility expand your thinking and not intended to convince you of anything. Please use any of the ideas in this book that might be of help to you. Otherwise ignore the ideas that don't fit you or make you feel right or are contrary to your current beliefs. Hopefully this book will provide you with a worthwhile and enjoyable experience.

Some of the daily quotes in this book are based our inner and sometimes unrealized constant desire for action. This desire for action was created within us so that we could maximize our learning experiences. This desire for action is fulfilled by us when we engage life and fully experience it, while having fun. Since our subconscious does not distinguish good from bad and only wants action, we may experience personal maladies and problems when that is the only way that our subconscious can obtain the action it wants and needs. Let's keep our thoughts and talk positive as we fully engage life, and we will collect and enjoy many worthwhile and exciting experiences.

The daily thoughts in this book are designed to help us get the most out of our learning experiences and have fun, since that is one of the primary reasons we are in this wonderful 3 D dimension.

Sometimes we need a little extra inspiration. I have added a thirteenth month in the daily thoughts section of this book to cover that possibility.

The monthly chapters of this book include some of my personal experiences and conclusions along with similar quotations from relevant outside experts. I have also included a second 13th month chapter to provide inspiration to investors and those looking for ways to manage and grow their resources. This chapter covers The Goose and Money, The Rule of 72 and The 6 1/2 % Rule.

This book is written in fractal format so that you have the option to skip around or read the book beginning to end or to follow the thoughts with your calendar. I hope that these daily and monthly thoughts will help you start your day in a positive way and help provide you with some ideas on how to make your life and day more interesting, exciting and fulfilling.

Paul William Johnson

DAILY
INSPIRATIONAL
THOUGHTS

JANUARY

1. There is much beauty in life that we don't recognize when we are focused on our fears or any form of negativity.

2. It is better to accept negative experiences for the lessons they teach us rather than thinking we are victims.

3. Never get lost in the roles you play in life whether in relationships, jobs or genders.

4. Rising to challenges is part of the purpose for our existence. This gives us a chance to use and expand our talents and abilities.

5. Another purpose for our existence is to learn how to use and focus our energy to create what we want.

6. Our outer ego frequently loses awareness of circumstances when it becomes caught up in strong emotions. We must learn to be masters of our emotions.

7. Never be captive to your fears and doubts because we do have the ability to release ourselves from them.

8. We are programed with taught thought. New information is sometimes dismissed because it does not fit into our taught thought. Always explore other possibilities when new information crosses your path.

9. There is plenty of everything. Never focus on the idea of limited abundance, lack or limitation because it leads to and keeps people in poverty.

10. It is important to be joyful because it depletes our energy when we are in fear, are unhappy or judgmental.

11. Memory patterns can be carried from lifetime to lifetime. That is why people come into this world with specific talents, likes and dislikes and different attitudes and beliefs.

12. Since people have different attitudes and beliefs, they can create a heaven or a hell out of the same event.

13. Keep your energy positive because whatever you resonate with will be revealed to you by your experiences.

14. We are focused in only one version of a magnificent reality although there are many.

15. Judgment is not necessary. When you consider that people select and create situations that provide them with maximum learning experiences, you will never judge them based on your standards or experiences.

16. Focus on your goals as already met and you will more effortlessly attain them. Focusing negatively on obstacles that stand in your way will reinforce and strengthen any negative condition.

17. Confidence is extremely important because it leads to more confidence.

18. Expectation is a creative force. If you expect danger or failure, you will help create it. Expect success and you will naturally create success.

19. The emotional power behind your expectations brings them into your experience.

20. Use your expectations more because they are creative and will help you form your abilities.

21. Your subconscious has wonderful tools that include experiences, information, talents and abilities from past lives that it uses when called upon in critical situations.

22. As much as possible keep your inner attitudes positive. It will then accept and attract positive experiences, while closing out others.

23. Your intellect, which gives you a great analysis of the 3D world, is part of your outer ego and not part of your inner creative ego.

24. If you direct your inner self to easily and joyfully steer you through your physical existence, it will do so. Focusing on difficulties blocks your inner self from doing so.

25. We experience only a small portion of the fantastic reality available to us.

26. Your attitude creates your possibilities and impossibilities.

27. We have creative abilities because there is a portion of All That Is (God) that resides within us as part of our inner self.

28. Every person is cherished by God who is aware of our significant and insignificant problems. If we ask for help from God, when needed, it will be provided along with the best way to maximize our learning experience.

29. Your inner self will teach you your planned lessons; it knows the best way to get its message across when you trust it.

30. When you enthusiastically and exuberantly project your energy outward, you will naturally create a fun and joyful existence.

31. Try to avoid self-pity and despair as an easy escape from taking responsibility to change a situation for the better. Taking ownership of the situation will give you the best results.

FEBRUARY

1. Insisting on prerequisites blinds us to the way life works. We must go with the flow.

2. Life accepted on its own terms will yield its secrets of joy, peace and exhilaration.

3. Avoid any thoughts of hate because hate continually creates destruction, unhappiness, and sorrow.

4. The energy that is within us is greater than we can imagine. When we use more energy engaging life, more energy will become available to us.

5. Laughing loudly or crying deeply releases pent up feelings.

6. Never take ownership of any regrets because the negative suggestions they create will constantly work against you.

7. Our roles in life are chosen by us. If we don't like them, we can change them.

8. Words are not as important as the message of the emotion behind them.

9. The emotion of joy or terror is reflected in our faces. Sorrow also has many faces.

10. Think in terms of abundance and it will lead to more success and abundance.

11. A sense of joy, fun and spontaneity is essential to enjoying a happy life.

12. People will remember how you made them feel. Help them to feel good and they will reflect that feeling back to you.

13. When we spontaneously and deliberately use our energy, we will be at the top of our profession, in excellent health and filled with abundance.

14. Our problems are not in exterior circumstances but in our mental attitudes toward them.

15. Your outer ego forgets itself when caught up in strong positive or negative emotions.

16. Never get lost in the roles (relationships, jobs and gender) you play in life. They are just situations you have chosen to maximize your learning experience.

17. Reach for the doughnut and not the hole. View your life from the blessings you do have rather than what you do not have.

18. Overcoming problems and adversities gives your life more meaning.

19. You can speed the creation of what you want by giving it more attention and focus.

20. There are hundreds of languages in the world, but a smile speaks all of them.

21. We successfully learn the power of creation by noticing the results of our thoughts, beliefs and emotions.

22. Accept your own worth as fantastic when you wake up in the morning by focusing on your accomplishments and positive learning experiences from the previous day along with the adventures of the day to come.

23. Look for the good in every situation since your feelings are based on your interpretation of the events you experience.

24. Truth is always colored by our perspective. When we keep our perspective positive, we will experience a more joyful and positive life.

25. We must deliberately focus on keeping our attitude and energy positive because low energy is the level of hate, envy, greed and never being satisfied.

26. The energy frequency at which we vibrate is directly related to the control we have over our thoughts, actions and emotions. It is important that we keep our energy frequency up because low energy results in frustration, discouragement and depression.

27. The human mind has almost unlimited creative ability that improves with every use. It is always ready and waiting for our call to action.

28. Whatever you think about and demand with passion and emotion will be brought into your experience by your subconscious mind. The whole process starts by first using your creative imagination.

29. "Imagination is everything. It is the preview of life's coming attractions." — Albert Einstein

MARCH

1. We need to keep on open mind because negative conditioning is so prevalent in those we encounter every day. Taking into consideration that they may be struggling with their learning experiences may help us to accept them and their negative attitudes.

2. Always look for new information to consider. This is because we may be programmed with "taught thought" that screens out information that does not conform to it.

3. We should be able to accept those that we disagree with without criticizing them. Criticism is a form of "taught thought".

4. Breathe deeply when you become fearful, or experience negative emotions and it will help remove them.

5. We can learn to master our judgments by interacting with those who don't have like minds. Just consider they are working on their learning experiences which are different from ours.

6. Your life is living itself and expressing itself through you. Your destiny is not your fate but can be changed by you.

7. When we choose acceptance and compassion for every event in our lives, the choice brings wisdom and peace profound.

8. An attitude of acceptance of the difficult situations in your life will lead to solutions and the best path to take through any difficulty. Owning and accepting your situation will provide you with the power to change it.

9. Never get lost in negativity, blaming others or yourself or your past for your difficulties. Just make the choice to find your way out of your difficulties and you will do so.

10. You will find that it is easy to resonate with some of the things you want to accomplish. Whatever you resonate with will be naturally attracted into your experience.

11. When we realize that we create every situation in our lives to learn, then it is easy to release any anger or judgment regarding those situations.

12. We are sometimes self-hypnotized to keep secrets from ourselves. These are the only secrets we must worry about. Occasionally we can learn these secrets from what others have to say about us.

13. Remember the feeling of the energy that pervades you when you are feeling good and are happy with your experience. Then transfer that feeling and energy into your unpleasant experiences.

14. Curiosity helps you explore the world and gets you into doing your thing.

15. Love yourself first. Then you will be able to love others more easily.

16. Avoid obligations because they can be an imposed belief for the benefit of others.

17. List and think about your positive beliefs and accomplishments and the negative ones will fade away.

18. No matter how tempted you are to look to others for advice, you are your own authority. Answers literally come from within yourself when you ask and believe that your inner self will make them available to you.

19. Our intent draws to us the circumstances and information we need to solve our problems and to answer our questions.

20. Our inner self whispers instructions through that "still small voice". We must listen.

21. Through our creations we recognize our abilities.

22. When we realize our thoughts form our reality, then we are no longer slaves to events.

23. Desire is a companion of success. What we strongly desire will attract what we need to get what we want. Our level of success is only limited by our imagination.

24. Within ourselves is the ability to face and enjoy each day as it comes.

25. When we try too hard, we push what we want away from us.

26. It is not what we think of as negative thoughts but our fear of them that creates more fear.

27. One form of happiness is when we engage and master our actions.

28. What a caterpillar calls the end is really change or the beginning of a new and exciting cycle. We have many cycles in our lives that change or end and new and more exciting cycles begin. Therefore, we should embrace, enjoy and never fear change.

29. When you fully engage life, it will become an exciting adventure.

30. Your comfort zone is a beautiful place, but nothing ever happens there.

31. We meet our beliefs in our experiences. We must learn to disregard beliefs that imply basic limitations.

APRIL

1. Self-talk is a form of self-hypnosis that we constantly give ourselves as a driver in the formation of our beliefs. These beliefs are then reflected in our daily experience.

2. We can reinforce our negative beliefs by concentrating on them to the exclusion of conflicting data. We will then bring them into our experience through natural hypnosis.

3. Any time we have the undivided attention of another, we act as a hypnotist.

4. If you use natural hypnosis ten minutes per day by visualizing that you already have what you want, you will get it. The point of power is always in the moment.

5. When we repeat repeatedly in our mind that we already have what we want, our subconscious will attempt to bring into our experience. This is because repetition is the law of the subconscious mind.

6. Belief in your personal worth helps increase the personal worth of others.

7. Always see the best in yourself and others and the best will be reflected to you.

8. Self-talk can be an asset to create what you want in your life because self-talk acts like the constant repetition of a hypnotist.

9. Never concentrate on your liabilities but concentrate on using your talents and abilities to get you where you want to go.

10. We are created to naturally seek greater realms of creativity and experience by engaging life, solving our problems, enjoying our successes and having fun.

11. Beginnings and endings are a reality in our 3D dimension because they maximize our learning experiences with before and aftereffects. In other dimensions, including the dream dimension, thought creation is instantaneous with no before and aftereffects.

12. Your physical body has a beginning, and it will have an end. The inner eternal you that occupies your physical body has never had a 3D beginning and will never have a 3D end.

13. Stay with your positive thoughts and attitudes and never use your imagination to prolong negative experiences. When negative thoughts and attitudes creep into your consciousness, simply imagine happy circumstance and the negative thoughts will disappear.

14. Only use your imagination to visualize that you have what you want, and you will get it.

15. Our beliefs attract and bring into our experience certain events instead of others. Beliefs in success and exhilarating experiences will help create them in our experience.

16. We can use our free will along with our beliefs to change any experience we don't like.

17. Our beliefs, which cause our experiences, are programmable and can be changed. When we wrongly accept our beliefs as a characteristic of reality itself, they become invisible and are difficult to change.

18. We are constantly sending and receiving telepathic information. We react to all telepathic information according to our beliefs about reality. Many people naturally tune out of telepathic interplay because it is not part of their beliefs.

19. Imagination gives mobility to our beliefs. The proper use of our imagination will propel ideas in the direction of our desires.

20. Your outer ego makes it possible to focus your intellect on the 3D dimension. Your intellect brings the correct outer information to your inner self.

21. Our outer ego causes us to interpret everything in the light of ourselves. We then become the center of our universe.

22. When the ego gets too self-centered, it no longer interprets outer information. Then our inner self will be unable to send us important data. This can result in turmoil for the individual who will do all the wrong things. The cure, which is difficult for many people, is to keep your thoughts focused positively until the outer ego realizes it is not in charge but a partner with your inner self.

23. We have inner senses that work in the inner dimensions when the outer senses are sleeping. Use these inner senses to explore your dreams and other dimensions.

24. We have a subconscious connection between our inner and outer senses. Since time and space do not exist in our inner senses, we can use them to communicate and provide guidance with "that still small voice", to telepathy the feelings we get from our inner self.

25. The space between imagination and attainment is filled by desire, expectation and focus. Filling that space helps us create what we want.

26. Never let your children believe in their deficiencies. Rather encourage them to use their strengths and abilities.

27. We each have responsibility for our own thoughts, beliefs and emotions and what we create with them.

28. Each day is a miracle to be explored.

29. No one can change your life but you. This is your personal salvation.

30. When you realize that your inner self naturally demands the best that is within you, you will exceed what you think is possible for you and understand that you have only scratched the surface of your potential.

MAY

1. You cannot compare yourself with others because you are one in billions and there is no one in the universe that has the same combination of talents and experiences that you have.

2. You have your own fantastic combination of beliefs. Separate your own beliefs from the beliefs of others. Then listen to your own experience and forget your taught thought.

3. Your accomplishments are your best builder of greater self-esteem and confidence.

4. When your fears are felt and faced, you will automatically bring about their resolution.

5. You must go beyond the obvious and the beliefs of the masses to think independently.

6. Be completely engaged in what you are doing, and you will accomplish your goals with ease.

7. There is a difference in being told things and knowing them. Knowing comes from within. When you know, you don't have to be told.

8. The fear of others causes us to put ourselves into their reality. Then we are forced to fight on their terms.

9. Desire, wish and expectation rule all actions and outcomes.

10. Growth and challenge are perceived not in terms of achievement but in terms of intensities and learning experiences.

11. If you have a problem or a question that needs to be answered, just relax or do something else and the answer will probably just pop into your mind.

12. Be open to emotions that unexpectedly flow through you. Just let them go and they should disappear, or the emotion may lead you to the belief that caused it.

13. Focusing on obstacles that stand in your way will reinforce the negative condition. Let the obstacles go and then go with the flow and you will be shown the best way around them.

14. You cannot escape your attitudes. They form what you see that will include your thoughts and attitudes materialized in physical form.

15. If you want to know what others think of you, then ask yourself what you think of others and you will have your answer.

16. Desire is to obtain what aspire is to achieve.

17. Every day is a gift to be explored, experienced and enjoyed in the moment. That is why it is called the present.

18. Curiosity helps you enjoy and experience the wonderful diversity in our world.

19. Your habits can work for or against you. Expand the good ones and eliminate the bad ones.

20. When you go all out for something, you will naturally generate the extra energy to make that thing easier to obtain.

21. We see only the version of reality we are focused on although there are many realities that exist concurrently.

22. We all have hidden talents that we can use. All we must do is try many things and those talents will become apparent when you excel at some of them.

23. Your best source of wisdom and advice is within you.

24. Trust and believe in yourself. It is a form of wisdom that will seem like magic.

25. Enthusiasm along with perseverance will help you reach your goals.

26. When we don't see opportunities, we must make them or let them find us through our expectations. Wise men make more opportunities than they find.

27. A variety of thoughts and experiences will make your life more interesting and exciting.

28. It is better to try and fail than to never try at all because our failures will lead us to success.

29. When you are faced with uncertainty, start doing and new paths will open.

30. First ask questions and you will have a good way to learn about anything.

31. The experience we gain from reaching our goal is more important than the goal itself because we can apply that same experience to reaching many future goals.

JUNE

1. What lies inside of us is more important than what lies outside of us because the outside is created from the inside.

2. We will only hear and see that which we experience and understand. The native Indians could not see the Mayflower until they were on it because they had never experienced a canoe that large.

3. Do it now. This clears our mind of clutter, eliminates tomorrow's priority list and frees up our tomorrow's fun time.

4. Adversity is more easily overcome when we focus on a new activity. Sometimes the solution just pops into our mind when we are doing something else.

5. Insight is understanding or knowledge. Sometimes it is better to get insight into a problem before blindly proceeding to solve it.

6. A life that is too busy has no time for fun and enjoyment. Eliminate activities that do not serve you well and you will have a more exciting life.

7. Too much idleness can lead to a multitude of problems since we were created for action.

8. A victim has given away his power to create his own destiny. Never give your power away but use it to create what you want.

9. Inner despair and depression are an indication that a person needs to find a way to better engage life and to continuously learn.

10. Consciousness evolved the physical body for the purpose of creating learning experiences and having fun. Let's do it!

11. When we strongly desire something, a path will open for us to attain it. Go for it!

12. Our lives work best when we maintain humor, think big and go for it!

13. The logical mind is a magnificent tool but when overtaxed, overused and abused, it creates anxiety and stress.

14. Making a change requires commitment, determination and willpower to bring it about.

15. The real purpose of civilization is to enable and teach us how to live with others in peace, joy, security and abundance.

16. When you are not feeling at total peace, this is a signal that there is judgment that needs to be released.

17. As we move toward inner guidance, our outer ego moves over to let our inner guidance system have more predominance in our lives.

18. Our body functions as a self-healing system when we do not let our fears, thoughts and beliefs interfere with its processes.

19. When you use statements, such as don't, not good at, can't etc., you add energy to what you don't want or can't do and bring it into your experience.

20. Live for today and your worries will go away.

21. We should help others only when they really need help, then they will learn self-reliance. When we do things for others that they could do for themselves, they will never learn.

22. Anger is about yourself not being able to control others. Just let others be and go with the flow and your anger will disappear.

23. Sometimes we must thoroughly evaluate and possibly select a person for something. This is different from personally criticizing a person. When we criticize, there is only downside for both parties.

24. You should always spend some time thinking about and appreciating your wonderful accomplishments. This will put out energy to bring you even greater accomplishments.

25. Some people literally and unknowingly center their lives around their maladies and problems when they are not able to stop talking about them. This extra energy and focus can only make their maladies and problems worse because it will make them grow and expand. Never talk about your maladies and problems and you will have a healthier and more satisfying life.

26. Whenever we describe something as difficult or something we can't do, we are ensuring that it will remain so in our reality.

27. When you have a strong desire to know something, simply ask your inner self and you will be led to the answer, or it will in some way be revealed to you.

28. Never accommodate others at the expense of yourself. In the big picture, only you are responsible for you.

29. Fear tethers you to what you fear. Stop giving energy to your fear by focusing on it. Change your focus away from your fear and the tether will go away.

30. Always focus on positive aspects and outcomes and you will create them.

JULY

1. When our inner expectations and our outer realities differ, we get angry. These differences need to be only temporary if we can look at them as a signal to do things differently or as a necessary adjustment to keep us on our best path.

2. Conflicts and anger are sometimes a method of communicating feelings between people. They can lead to a solution, an understanding of each position or a compromise when both parties want a solution.

3. The human personality has no limits, except those it accepts. By accepting that anything is possible, we open the door to unlimited success.

4. Inspiration does not come from our outer ego but from our inner self. It comes when we have a strong desire to accomplish something.

5. Keep your thoughts positive. We lose two ways with negative or destructive thoughts. First, negative thoughts attract more negativity. Second, we rob ourselves of the positive elements of life including happiness when we focus on destructive thoughts.

6. Our attitude toward what is possible determines what is possible for us.

7. Our attitude creates possibilities and impossibilities. If something is not working for us, then if we change our attitude toward it, it will work.

8. Always love, appreciate and have confidence in yourself. Never indulge in self-pity because it can be highly destructive and dissipate your energy.

9. The intensity of an experience rather than its duration in time will determine its effect on you and become part of your eternal experiences.

10. We create our realities from our expectations. We must deal with these realities, or we must change them.

11. Fear cannot be ignored. It must be faced and conquered before it leads to retreat.

12. Never focus on fear because it can negatively impact your life when fear is anticipated.

13. Never concentrate on or worry about physical symptoms of an illness or you may attract the real illness. Our bodies are created to heal themselves when we do not put obstacles like worrying about symptoms in their path.

14. The exploration of inner space is one of our life's mission's. This exploration will expand our experiences and make our lives more fulfilling.

15. The intensity of a feeling, whether good or bad, can dominate your experience. Enjoy the good ones and do the opposite when you feel failure, hatred, resentment or fear.

16. Joy will emerge from within you, when needed, by recalling joyful situations. Pure joy can literally change the direction of your life.

17. When negative images come into your consciousness, replace them with positive ones. Then you will be giving more energy to positive experiences and attract more of them into your life.

18. We must keep our thoughts and attitudes positive because we cannot escape them, and they will form the nature of what we see. What we see is really our own thoughts and attitudes materialized.

19. Telepathy operates at a subconscious level. When we continually think a person will respond to us in a certain way, we are constantly sending that person a telepathic suggestion that they do so. Then we shouldn't be surprised when they respond to us that way. Focus on the best in people and they will give you their best.

20. When you inadvertently create what you fear, your creation will make you think your fears are justified.

21. Never drive yourself to prove that others are lazy or inadequate at what they do. We all have different talents and abilities that makes it impossible to compare people.

22. Try working with your hands to see if you enjoy it. Many have creativity that is expressed through their hands. This may include artwork, healing, cooking or building things.

23. Have faith in your abilities because they represent freedom and eventual success in whatever you may try.

24. True success comes from your own efforts. Other successes will fade and have very little meaning to you.

25. Each goal we reach gives us strength and the ability to achieve additional goals that are more difficult.

26. Demand more of yourself and you will do even greater things.

27. Live every day to its fullest and do not be a slave to the future. If we do not learn to enjoy today, we will not be able to enjoy the future, no matter what it may bring.

28. There is no easy way; the way that seems easiest is the hardest way of all.

29. We should never be afraid of failure. Sometimes we need failure as a steppingstone or learning experience to reach goals that would have otherwise been unattainable.

30. No one owes us anything. We owe everything to ourselves.

31. Don't look for windfalls. Our own abilities will better provide everything we want.

AUGUST

1. Most people know but a small part of their inner self. However, our inner self knows us well and guides our actions, whether or not we intellectually realize its presence.

2. Even though disasters and hopelessness are an inevitable part of our lives, we should not focus too much on them. This is because there is little upside to negative focus, and it has the potential to disrupt our mental health and our feeling of wellbeing. It is best for most people to find a diversion and accept disasters as part of our life's experience.

3. Full freedom is best reached when we face our responsibilities. Then we can use our natural abilities and all our potential to fulfill our responsibilities.

4. We can expect help from the Master Within or All That Is (God) if we ask for it. We should not act on faith alone because we will eventually get some evidence that help is on the way.

5. If you can trust your inner self, you will find out that you have more knowledge, ability and information available to you than you might have thought possible.

6. We are not always aware of what is best for us on a conscious level. We need to be flexible and want what is best for our own development and the development of others. Then the way will come to us more effortlessly.

7. Our true fantastic identity is within us, and we should not look for it by imitating others. Others cannot give us a sense of worth.

8. Think in terms of plenty of everything and you will find plenty in material, financial and other areas. Thoughts of want will produce want and will justify that want.

9. We have inner senses that allow us to perceive the reality of inner existence. We all use our inner senses when we dream or visualize.

10. Knowledge cannot be given; it must be experienced.

11. Never fear to let go of something that is not working for you. This frees up your energy to try something else.

12. One of the rules of the 3D dimension is that we must forget that we are playing a game. This helps us to completely engage the 3D dimension so that we can maximize our fun and learning experiences.

13. In non-time dimensions such as dreaming, your thoughts are instantly created. If you don't like a dream, then ask your dream self to take you to a better dream or a safe place and it will. In other dimensions, your thoughts are always your protection.

14. Our physic abilities such as intuition, telepathy, following inner direction, healing etc., will grow if we decide to use them.

15. All possibilities and probabilities have their origin in non-time. That is why physic readings are only probabilities that can be influenced by free will.

16. There is a difference between being told things and knowing them. Knowing comes from within and we all use some of that knowledge whether we realize it or not.

17. Our inner self possesses all answers and will give us answers if we trust, believe and expect it will.

18. The more you use your inner senses, the more energy and data you will have at your command that can be translated into behavior and knowledge. Then it can become part of your wisdom in your life adventure.

19. If you are feeling tense and can't let go of that feeling, hold a potato and feel the tension pass from your fingers to the potato which is a root vegetable. You will experience that the potato does know how to draw tension out of you.

20. Problems only appear to be exterior circumstances but have their origin in your mental attitude and habitual thoughts. Work on breaking habitual thoughts and attitudes and your problems will began to disappear.

21. Your value does not increase with financial success. Underestimation of your own worth can lead to overestimation of the value of your financial worth. There is no reason why we can't pay more attention to our own worth and be balanced and successful at both.

22. When we take responsibility to expand our awareness to use more of our abilities, it will be easier for us to communicate with our fellow human beings.

23. Our consciousness only occupies our physical body and is independent of it. Creativity is one of the most important attributes of consciousness.

24. Our inner self feeds our outer ego only with those feelings, emotions and data it can handle. When we push ourselves to our limits, our limits will expand along with our learning experiences.

25. The laws of our inner universes are not bound by the 3D universe laws of logic and take no time. Our inner universes include energy transformation, durability and creation.

26. Whatever we think about we create. To get outside our universe, we must travel inward.

27. When our outer ego understands the value of the inner self, its limitations began to dissipate along with close rapport to make your life more interesting and exciting.

28. Hypnotism is a tool to release the conscious personality from its restrictive and limiting beliefs. It allows the conscious personality to change its focus to other dimensions which increases your inner awareness. It is much safer than drugs

when used to expand your awareness because you are always in control.

29. Complicated relationships are an attempt to grow or learn in the face of difficulties that seem insurmountable. When both parties began to focus on the 95% of the things they like about the other person instead of the 5% of the things they don't like, the relationships will improve.

30. Let's be like children who believe that each tomorrow will be rewarding and filled with discovery; then we can have that experience also.

31. We have incredible power within us. All the knowledge about ourselves, our challenges and problems that we will ever need to know, lies within us.

SEPTEMBER

1. Thoughts thrive on association. They attract others like themselves and repel thoughts threatening to their survival. Let's put plenty of good thoughts out there and enjoy what they attract.

2. Go with the flow and enjoy the natural goodness of your day. Do not be like people who try to be good because they think they are bad or unworthy and want to compensate for it.

3. Myths and symbols are often closer to reality than "hard facts" because people tend to only see the facts that support their position and are blind to the rest.

4. True spirituality is a thing of joy and spiritual adventure with your inner self. It is the sense of joy that makes all creativity possible.

5. Follow your emotions that you do not like back to your beliefs. You will then be led to the beliefs behind the emotion. Then change the belief to what you want, and your emotional reaction will also change.

6. Your conscious mind directs the flow of your experience through your beliefs.

7. No problems mean no growth. Always consider your problems as opportunities for growth. Ask the question: What do I need to do differently to create a learning experience that eliminates this problem?

8. Your life will be fuller if you discover and use more of your abilities. We all have hidden abilities we need to discover and use.

9. We are in this physical existence to learn and understand that our energy, translated into feelings, thoughts, beliefs and emotions, causes all experiences.

10. Our individuality is never lost but becomes part of the inner self that includes a composite of all egos from previous incarnations. Some egos will split off and become their own inner self if they so desire. That is why different close entities can trace their lineage back to when they were one entity.

11. Look beyond people's thoughts and see their needs and it will be easier to love them and see their natural abilities.

12. Never give conscious consideration to events you don't want to occur, and you will reduce the possibility of them occurring.

13. Never concentrate your thoughts and attention on areas of your least satisfaction because they will act as a deepening hypnotic suggestion to keep them coming into your experience.

14. When you focus your attention on what you want, it pulls energy away from what you don't want.

15. The intensity of conscious concentration blocks out barriers and allows the message to go directly to our subconscious where it is acted upon. Let's use our concentration to create what we want.

16. We should never judge people based on our standards and experiences because they have selected specific situations to provide themselves with maximum learning experiences.

17. We should never tell ourselves we are feeling fine when we hurt. Just accept the responsibility for your condition and ask yourself what you need to do to change it and what do you need to learn from this situation.

18. Savor your good moments and this will extend your joyful feeling.

19. Our outer ego accepts only a few of our natural abilities. When we discover and use more of our natural abilities, our ego self will jump on board and will enjoy them with us.

20. We can work out solutions to problems in the dream state by asking ourselves to dream about the problem and provide us solutions as we wake up or lead us to the best solution.

21. It makes no difference whether the time, history and other events are correct as we are told by experts. The important thing is that we believe and experience them as if they are the truth because our beliefs create our reality.

22. Suggestions to program your belief system work best just before you go to sleep. Repeat positive suggestions and they will start appearing in your experiences.

23. Telepathy and clairvoyance occur more readily in the dream state. We can transfer this information to our outer senses by recording our thoughts on our iPhones the first thirty seconds after we wake up.

24. Your attitude speaks louder than what you say. If your attitude is not uplifting and supportive of others, this is all other people will remember about you. By keeping your attitude positive, this will help and not hinder you in your interactions with others.

25. Goals are important because they keep the target of what we want in focus. Many times, when we focus on the target, our subconscious will set up the easiest way for us to attain it. It will be as if providence keeps crossing our path.

26. We cannot take risks and try new things without having some failures. We should consider failures as learning experiences that are part of the cost of business of succeeding in life.

27. Life is a series of fun times and learning experience. Learning experiences are personal and can only be understood by those learning them.

28. We must never demand answers but let them come to us.

29. Our beliefs create our experiences. We can remove our negative beliefs and replace them with positive beliefs. Then our experiences will be more positive.

30. Our sleeping dreams have complete freedom from physical space and time. We can tell ourselves to remember the important points when we first wake up. We also have lucid dreams where we are awake and know that we are dreaming. We can then direct our inner self to take us where we can find what we want to know or experience.

OCTOBER

1. We should always treat others the way we would like to be treated because it will bring out the best in them. Then we both will have a wonderful experience.

2. Keep your emotional attitudes positive because they will be reflected in your behavior.

3. A person's attitude reflects their feelings about a given subject. This will tell us more about that person than their words.

4. The power of our individual self is unlimited. The only limits we have are those we inadvertently place upon ourselves.

5. A universal law that applies to all dimensions is that energy follows the focus of our thoughts and is creative. Let's use our thoughts to create what we want.

6. The contrast between what we consider positive and negative attracts our attention and keeps our lives from becoming boring.

7. To be successful at anything, we need to be able to perceive things about to happen. This will give us the ability to change course or make corrections before it is too late.

8. We need to act in the moment when we get that strong gut feeling and not wait to over-analyze the situation and miss the opportunity.

9. Become aware of your beliefs because belief is an attitude of the mind that determines the course of your life.

10. The real you will be reflected in your thoughts. Get to know yourself better by becoming more aware of your thoughts.

11. When we focus on our responsibility to develop our abilities and to materialize our potential, exciting new worlds will open to us.

12. There is much useful telepathic information available to us if we can get into the habit of going with our first thought. Going with our first thought will make it easier to understand those who cross our path.

13. Our reality is what we live in that is created with our thoughts and beliefs. This is more important than actuality or what is because we are not focused there.

14. Accept your failures head on and turn them into successes. Never even lean toward denial because it will make you feel unworthy.

15. Your expectations alone can be an be an asset to assist you in feelings of joy. What about that fun trip or event you will be going to?

16. Life is naturally abundant, vigorous and strong. People react to negative suggestions only when their own attitudes are negative. Let's jump on life's positive train anytime we are feeling down.

17. By the law of compounding, we can become creators of wealth rather than destroyers of wealth by accumulating debt.

18. When we sleep and dream, everything is possible because our reasoning mind with its rigid beliefs is asleep. Let's carry those dream possibilities back into our waking life.

19. It is up to us to examine our beliefs and change those beliefs that don't serve us. Our beliefs should include that we have the right to be happy, to express our creativity and to trust and believe in ourselves.

20. Our universe is a dynamic motion propelled by a vital life force that permeates everything. When that motion is disrupted by a static life doing nothing, those people will become depressed, anxious and fearful. Engage life to its fullest and you will be in sync with that vital life force.

21. Most people live in a world of lack and limitation and don't think big enough. They focus on what is wrong and why things can't be done. There is magic in thinking big and living in your own world of positive thinking and beliefs.

22. There are strong group thoughts that enter our consciousness at athletic events, political rallies/protests, Christmas, tragedies etc. Enjoy the positive ones and ignore the negative ones.

23. Everything in our 3D universe is spirit that occupies a physical form. Every life form exists in time and space to gather information and experience. It then returns to spirit to complete its cycle. Have a great ride in your present cycle.

24. You can speed up the creation of something you want simply by giving it more attention. Your subconscious will do the rest.

25. One of the keys to manifestation is to focus your thoughts powerfully and persistently enough to eliminate distractions.

26. Money and prosperity have a pattern. The pattern of the wealthy is that they live on uncertainty and take risks because they have confidence in their ability to overcome uncertainty. This type of pattern can also be used by you to create prosperity in your life.

27. We have more power available to us than we can ever realize. Think of the power of any emotion and watch what it can accomplish. When we focus on our passions, our ability to accomplish them will get stronger.

28. Go all out for what you want, otherwise you will never know how much you can accomplish.

29. The first step in fulfilling our dreams is to clearly define what we want. Give your dream energy. Think about it, talk about it, sleep on it, share it, give it voice and sing it. Then it will be realized quicker than you think.

30. Music has a pattern. It has measures, notes, beats, crescendos/decrescendos and time signatures. All things in life also have patterns for us to experience and enjoy.

31. Our personal world is impacted by our perceptions. Never perceive your problems as difficulties but perceive them as opportunities to learn by succeeding at solving them.

NOVEMBER

1. Desire is a common trait in all of us. However, if we are long on desire and short on diligence, we will find it difficult to fulfill our desires. Let's diligently focus on creating what we want and we will get it.

2. A good leader instinctively knows when to lead and when to follow. The synergism and motivational power of a good leader is almost unimaginable. Let's be ready to step into a leadership role when the opportunity presents itself.

3. Our belief system can be programed through the subconscious mind by emotionally charged states, by being in a relaxed state, or by repetition. Let's program some positive successes and what we want through repetition into our subconscious mind.

4. Our conscious mind sees from cause to effect while our subconscious mind works from effect to cause. The effects are our goals. Let's repeat them repeatedly and let our subconscious find ways to bring them to us.

5. The butterfly effect explains how small changes can change the outcome of larger patterns. Always consider that small changes in your business or personal life can make large changes in bigger patterns and outcomes.

6. Patience is a state of existence where we can instantly access the subconscious or the flow or being in the zone. Let's practice more patience and see how it makes our life more successful.

7. Application of knowledge is wisdom. We must experience knowledge and internalize it before it becomes wisdom. Let's more fully experience life and we will gain more wisdom.

8. Life can be a great joy when you automatically take responsibility for your choices and make corrections as you go.

9. We live in a world of illusion because we are not prepared in advance to see through the many illusions we encounter in our daily lives. We then accept what we see as the truth. It is wise to take inventory of our belief filters and decide which illusions serve us and which ones serve others.

10. When we trust our intuition, it will allow us to be in the right place at the right time and do the right thing at the right time.

11. I can't say enough times that if we can be passionate about something, we will never be depressed and will experience life to its fullest.

12. There is an old Eskimo saying that says. "If you are not lead dog, your view never changes". Those who do not lead experience a very limited life. Keep taking the lead in your business and professional life and you will see an amazing world that is seen by just a few.

13. What is Real Awareness? One of the first steps in the mastery of awareness is to recognize that much of what we believe has been programed into us. There is great freedom to be experienced once you have cleaned out the garbage put into your mind by others.

14. We are continuously plugged into electronic devices of all kinds. Nobody notices that the devices hypnotize us and program our minds. These devices can even program us on what to eat and drink. We need to unplug from the programmed beliefs and use our own real choices to create the life we want.

15. There is plenty of everything and it is ours for the asking. We need to keep our belief systems programmed to supply our fondest dreams and wishes and programed to the fact that we can create whatever we want.

16. Much small talk degenerates into one upmanship. Get into the habit of not getting into that type of discussion. Mentally ask yourself "what are they really saying", "what do they want", "how do they feel" etc. Then notice the first thought that pops into your mind and it will tell you.

17. We experience the Force when we feed our subconscious positive thoughts. These thoughts then go out in front of us to balance our activities and to help us control the events in our lives.

18. The more you love, respect and value yourself, the easier it will be to get the force to flow and work through you.

19. Your thinking is your mind's programming letting you know what it believes about everything.

20. Focusing energy can be called attention. Attention is a powerful tool that can either work for or against you. Pay attention to what is wonderful and what is working in your life, and you will attract more of it.

21. The solution to most questions and problems lies within us and not from some outside source. Our lives are a mirror of where we are placing our attention. Just stop thinking sometime

and let the creative ideas and solutions start popping into your mind.

22. Once we know that we have done our very best, then we can let the judge in our logical minds take a permanent vacation.

23. Determination to never quit until we get what we want will give us the mental confidence to swim out and meet our ship when it had never intended to come into our port.

24. What most people consider thinking is just parroting, repeatedly, what other people have put into their minds. We need to make sure that we are doing our own thinking because we become slaves to those we inadvertently depend on to do our thinking.

25. If you want to stop the chatter that goes on in your mind, concentrate on and send love to someone you love and you will in effect be loving them instead of chattering.

26. Many plants and animals patiently wait for their pray and then ambush them. We can do the same thing by focusing our subconscious on bringing us the prey (goal and objectives) we want, and it will faithfully do so.

27. We are eternal spiritual beings occupying a physical body in order to create learning experiences, have fun and enjoy the physical world. When we think of the many electronic signals that cannot be physically observed, but still exist, it is easier to understand our wonderful nonphysical reality.

28. We are all subject to a herd instinct where we naturally want to follow the herd. The herd only follows (sometimes over a cliff), it never leads. We become successful by using our creative abilities that function outside the herd mind or instinct.

29. Once our belief system is programmed with certain beliefs, our subconscious will only let us see things that support that belief. When you think about the negative side of a person, just think the opposite and your subconscious will only show you the wonderful positive characteristics of that person.

30. One reason why most people don't follow through with their dreams is that they are afraid of failure. My greatest failures have led to my greatest successes and brought me to where I am today. When you have dreams, just follow them and they will take you to unimaginable experiences.

DECEMBER

1. Resistance is a rebellion in your belief system to the flow of life as it is. Let go of that resistance and go with the flow and you will more easily get to where you want to go.

2. In our personal or business life, we must focus on growth and maintaining it. When we are not in a growth cycle, we need to change our focus to efficiency. This will make us more competitive and ready for our next growth cycle.

3. Jack Nicholas once said that "people only do their best at things they truly enjoy". I think that this works because we will be so focused on the process of what we are doing that nothing else will matter. Enjoyment has no anxiety or fear and helps you trust yourself and have confidence in your abilities. Let's make sure we enjoy what we are doing, and we will succeed at it.

4. When athletes play their game, they don't work at it, they play. One way to be successful at what we do is to change our attitude from work to play. Then make work a game and play your game.

5. You don't drink beer, you rent it. Five minutes later you are in the restroom giving it back. Many good things in life are just

like that. Enjoy things when you can. When something goes well, give yourself a pat on the back and do something special.

6. Creation requires a clear image or a plan to determine where we want to go or what we want to create. We must allow our imagination to see our inward experience as a success before there is any physical evidence of success. Then there will be physical evidence when time catches up with us.

7. Many have the mistaken idea that finding out what others think on the internet will help them make their best decisions. At best, it will confirm their current beliefs. Our best answers come from within through intuitive thinking.

8. By becoming aware that we continuously learn from each other, we will discover that there is no one in our lives that we may encounter that does not have something to teach us.

9. The cockroach theory says that when we encounter one, there will always be more. This can be applied to many situations that range from stocks to pests. The important message for us is to dig deeper into situations we want to change.

10. We live life in many wonderful small worlds that are all part of our big world. These worlds could include music, sports,

professions, jobs etc. In these small worlds we can have wonderful experiences with others who have a common passion.

11. Excellence is a never-ending journey where we are always in a state of becoming better. Excellence is a satisfying component of any of life's journey.

12. When we go all out to engage life, we are placing a high value on our lives because we will accomplish great things.

13. Wu Wei says to respond to the true demands of situations, which tend only to be noticed when we put our own ego-driven plans aside.

14. Some valuable things in life cannot be achieved by simply trying harder, such as happiness and love.

15. It is never too late to enjoy our magnificent world. Being in my eighties, I find no end to the wonderful things I love to do, including writing. Keep engaging life and your life will keep engaging you and getting better.

16. No matter what our age, learning something new can aways be an exciting experience that will be ours forever.

17. When we turn our attention to positive thoughts, positive experience or music, it will naturally increase our physical energy.

18. Our inner self sometimes sends us messages in dreams about issues or things in our waking lives we need to change or things that we have ignored or repressed. Just face these issues and new ways will open to resolve them.

19. We are sometimes like iPhones when taking a photo because we only see and experience what we are focused on. There are many other exciting dimensions available to us, if we can first believe they exist and then focus on them.

20. The "Christmas Carol" by Charles Dickens, is a story about how Scrooge visited his past, present and future. What he saw made him want to change his future. We can also examine our past and use the present to create our future or to change our future if we want to make it better.

21. The Poet Rumi once said, "Set your life on fire and seek those that fan your flames".

22. When you wake up in the morning, get ready for the exciting and unanticipated events that will unfold in your magnificent day. Then every day will have the possibility of being the best day in your life.

23. The holiday season is a good time to focus on our blessings and to share ourselves and our joy with others.

24. Christmas Eve is a good time to get around the piano with your family and sing those old time Christmas and holiday carols.

25. As a federal holiday, people of all walks of life and religions can enjoy Christmas Day.

26. We easily understand the lessons of life in hindsight, but we create our future experiences in the present moment where all our creative abilities lie.

27. In looking back on the past year, what we have done or accomplished is not nearly as important as where we are this very moment and where we want to go this coming year.

28. "The secret of change is to focus all of your energy, not on fighting the old, but on building the new." – Socrates

29. By reflecting on your successes and failures of this past year, you will be building the foundation for your accomplishments this coming year.

30. New Year's resolution: Whatever we put off last year, we will accomplish this year along with the seizing some of the many new and exciting opportunities that will cross our path.

31. Happy New Year! Tomorrow will begin a new chapter and a new verse to add to your already fantastic and fulfilling book of life.

THE THIRTEENTH MONTH

For those that need extra inspiration.

1. You get what you concentrate on. There is no more important rule.

2. Live in the present moment as much as possible because everything happens there.

3. When your thoughts touch on your problems, imagine the best possible outcome. See your solution as already accomplished in your mind's eye. Then recall a feeling of accomplishment and joy when your problem was solved. This will help you attract the best solution.

4. What we change inwardly will also change in our outer reality.

5. Never be so impatient to express your own ideas that you forget to listen to others.

6. Demand the best that is within you. Then you will become more than you realize you can be.

7. Follow your feelings for they will lead you to your beliefs. Change your beliefs and you change your reality.

8. Direct knowledge is always available to those who can focus on desire, intent, love and belief.

9. Our impulses are one of our closest communications with our inner self.

10. We cannot love anybody until we can first love ourselves. Negative beliefs are a big hindrance to loving ourselves and others.

11. We are ever changing and never static. We are not the same person we were days or years ago.

12. We need to continuously develop our abilities and expand our experiences. We will then acquire a sense of purpose and our zest for life will increase.

13. When our life lacks excitement, we become depressed and are easily frustrated. We will then focus more on disasters and only see the bad in our world. This is a signal that we need to develop our purpose and abilities. Then our excitement for life will come back to us.

14. When we accept life's challenges, life will produce more excitement, more creativity and a zest for living.

15. When we rely on ourselves and allow our impulses more freedom, we will experience greater power and purpose to meet our goals.

16. Our inner self needs action to grow and expand. Action does not discriminate between painful and enjoyable. Have goals and a purpose and you will be led to positive enjoyable action.

17. Be decisive. Indecision is caused by fear.

18. Desire, focus and expectations are the basis for all realities and rule all actions.

The Thirteenth Month

19. Life is abundant, vigorous and strong. We have a natural defense against negative suggestions if we don't put blocks in the way.

20. We have no limitations or boundaries except those we accept out of ignorance.

21. We are here to participate in physical reality, operate in and experience it, develop our abilities, learn, create, solve problems and help others.

22. We must examine our beliefs because we create reality according to our beliefs and expectations.

23. Hypnosis is an exercise in the alteration of beliefs. Hypnosis clearly shows that the sense of experience follows expectations.

24. Our personal world is a replica of our thoughts and beliefs. Let's keep them positive and live in a magnificent world.

25. Your eternal soul is the most highly motivated, most energized and most potent consciousness known in any universe.

26. When you form artificial guilt in your mind, then it becomes a reality for you that must be worked out.

27. All events in your life, in hindsight, will be seen as creating the best learning experiences for you. Although it may not seem so at the time.

28. We draw to ourselves those values upon which we concentrate our attention.

29. We must trust that all the elements of experience are used for the greater good.

30. We have acquired our beliefs through self-hypnotism or being hypnotized by others.

31. We have a programmable belief system in order to create an infinite variety of experiences.

MONTHLY THOUGHTS FOR THE YEAR

JANUARY

The Month of Ambition

Your ambition is ignited when you have a strong purpose or goal you want to achieve. Your ambition, when focused within you, creates a successful path to achieve success to obtain what you want. Ambition then becomes the action that brings them into physical existence.

Your strong desire to be successful is a huge motivator and will jump-start your ambition. Your continued strong desire will keep the fires of your ambition going.

As you travel through your life's journey, your ambition will make it easier to experience the lessons you have chosen to learn. It will also help you develop your talents and abilities and will be the power to get you where you want to go. Ambition will also help you experience the real joy of life you are meant to experience. Then you can enjoy the exhilarating emotions of fun and accomplishment that leads to personal satisfaction and fantastic success.

In hindsight you will see that your ambition has taught you that your struggles and your sometimes difficulties to succeed are blessings because overcoming them will increase your self- esteem and the enjoyment of your life's journey.

Ultimate success in life comes from our inner guidance system that includes our inner drive and inner ambition that will help us to create what we want.

Never be lazy or lay around too much or it will suck the life out of your ambition. Ambitiously engage life and life will engage you to do your thing.

We must always use our ambition in a way that benefits ourselves and others. Ambition focused on a goal that justifies any means to attain it should never be acceptable. We see this in the horrors of war, in dictators, in bosses and leaders that bully their constituents. We may also see leaders and others that work hard to suppress the ambition of their opponents while other leaders will enhance the ambitions of those that support them.

In summary, ambition means we are naturally driven to achieve our goals and successes. It also means that we need to stay committed, even during hard times and adversity. Ambition is more important to your success than talents or resources because it is the driving force that leads you to succeed at whatever you desire. Ambition can also mean that you stay driven, by never giving up until you reach your goal or a better goal.

This month see if you can include using your ambition to help you to easily get to where you want to go or to keep you going to reach a goal you want to achieve.

Quotes on ambition:

A man's worth is no greater than the worth of his ambitions
  --Marcus Aurelius.

Keep away from those who try to belittle your ambitions. Small people always do that, but the really great make you believe that you too can become great.
  – Mark Twain

The people who are crazy enough to think they can change the world are the ones who do.
  -- Steve Jobs

Ambition is the path to success. Persistence is the vehicle you arrive in.
  --Bill Bradley

Great ambition is the passion of a great character.
  --Napoleon Bonaparte

Intelligence without ambition is a bird without wings.
  --Salvadori Dali

Ambition is enthusiasm with a purpose.
  --Frank Tyger

Ambition is more than pure desire. It is desire plus incentive –
determination – will to achieve that desire.
   --Herbert Armstrong

All Quotes are from brainyquotes.com

FEBRUARY

The Month of Curiosity

Curiosity is a strong desire to know or learn something and is one of the best ways to keep your mind active and not be too passive. Curious people always ask questions and search for answers. Their minds are always active. Since the mind is like a muscle which becomes stronger through continual exercise, the mental exercise caused by curiosity makes your mind stronger and stronger.

Curiosity is when you ask yourself the question "what's this?" or "how does this work?", when you see or think about something you don't understand. Curiosity can also put you on a path that leads to new discoveries as it has with entrepreneurs and those discovering better ways to do things. Walt Disney has said, "We keep moving forward, opening new doors, and doing new things, because we're curious and curiosity keeps leading us down new paths".

Curiosity asks questions that help us see new possibilities and insights that would have otherwise gone unnoticed. Questions can serve as the fuel for creativity which can lead to discovering and using our natural talents. Our questions must also be open ended and begin with «how» or «why».

These questions will help us to understand the answers we find.

If you want or need to learn something new, you can first survey the unknown subject by asking yourself or writing down questions. Next focus on those questions and trust your inner self to lead you to finding the answers. You will be led to the answers whether from within or from without. You will discover that answers from sometimes unlooked for places will help you to find what you want to know about the subject.

Intellectual curiosity is very important! We see that in how it manifests itself in geniuses like Thomas Edison, Leonardo da Vinci and Albert Einstein, who were all very curious.

Curiosity is an important way for you to develop your talents. Successful students and people who are successful after college often display a good measure of intellectual curiosity.

Curiosity so important because:

1. It makes your mind active instead of passive

Curious people always ask questions and search for answers. Their minds are always active.

2. It makes your mind observant of new ideas

When you are curious about something, your mind expects and anticipates new ideas related to the subject. When the ideas come, you will recognize them. Without curiosity, the ideas may pass right in front of you, and you will miss them because your mind is not prepared to recognize them. Just think: how many great ideas may have been lost due to lack of curiosity?

3. It opens new worlds and possibilities

By being curious you will be able to see new worlds and possibilities that are normally not visible. They are hidden behind the surface of normal life, and it takes a curious mind to look beneath the surface and discover these new worlds and possibilities.

4. It brings excitement into your life

The lives of curious people are far from boring. They are not dull or routine. New things will attract the curious person's attention.

5. It keeps you completely engaged in life which it considers an exciting adventure.

Some ideas to develop your curiosity:

1. Keep an open mind. Be open to learn, unlearn, and relearn. Some things you think you know and believe might not be working for you. Be prepared to accept this possibility and change your mind.

2. Don't take things at face value.

You will only see what you expect to see. If you accept what you see without trying to dig deeper, you will certainly lose your curiosity.

3. Ask questions relentlessly.

Ask questions: What is that? Why is it made that way? When was it made? Who invented it? Where does it come from? How does it work? What, why, when, who, where, and how.

4. Never consider anything as boring.

Whenever you think something as boring, you close one more door of possibilities. Curious people will not call something boring. They will see it as a door to an exciting new world.

Quotes on curiosity:

The important thing is not to stop questioning. Never lose a holy curiosity.
   --Albert Einstein

Curiosity is lying in wait for every secret.
   --Ralph Waldo Emerson

Once we believe in ourselves, we can risk curiosity, wonder, spontaneous delight, or any experience that reveals the human spirit.
   --E. E. Cummings

Satisfaction of one's curiosity is one of the greatest sources of happiness in life.
   --Linus Pauling

Curiosity is, in great and generous minds, the first passion and the last.
   --Samuel Johnson

Learning is by nature curiosity... prying into everything, reluctant to leave anything, material or immaterial, unexplained.
   --Philo

Curiosity is the engine of achievement
   --Ken Robinson

Critical thinking and curiosity are the key to creativity.
--Amala Akkinei

MARCH

The Month of Desire

Desire is a conscious impulse toward something that promises enjoyment or satisfaction in its attainment. It can also be a strong feeling of wanting to have something or wishing for something to happen.

Desire or wanting something can create good motivation toward getting it and can be the driving forces behind everything we do. It can be considered the foundation of most of our achievements. Desire is an essential starting point to establish a goal that we want to achieve.

Willpower is the necessary fuel to keep our desires going toward our goals. Commitment will keep us focused on them.

We can have the wind at our backs when we use our inner guidance system and go with the flow. This will be experienced by providence falling in our path and doors opening when we need them.

One obstacle that may weaken our desires is procrastination. A seemingly small task when put off may turn out to have been the task that was most vital to our success. One way to stop procrastination in its tracks is to adopt a "do it now" philosophy.

When we desire something, we need to decide if it is what we need or what we want. Needs are easier to focus on creating and wants may be easier to attract obstacles. Both are obtainable but wants may require more effort.

My grandmother gave me a book called <u>Secret of the Ages</u> for Christmas when I was 12 years old. It covered the law of attraction, the conscious and subconscious mind, see yourself doing it, as a man thinketh, the law of supply and many other ideas that I have used throughout my lifetime.

Finally, when we use our imagination to visualize our goals as already accomplished, we will be using one of our most creative and powerful tools to get what we want.

This month, see how many of your creative tools, including desire and imagination, you can use to create what you want in your life.

Quotes on desire:

I prefer to be a dreamer among the humblest, with visions to be realized, than lord among those without dreams and desires.
  --Khalil Gibran

One that desires to excel should endeavor in those things that are in themselves most excellent.
  --Epictetus

Whatever it is your heart desires, please go for it, it's yours to have.
  --Gloria Estefan

A strong, successful man is not the victim of his environment. He creates favorable conditions. His own inherent force and energy compel things to turn out as he desires.

--Orson Sweet Marden.

Desire is action. In the inner world, your desires bring about their own fulfillment, effortlessly. That inner world, and the exterior one, intersect and interweave. They only appear separate. In the physical world, time may have to elapse, or whatever. Conditions may have to change, or whatever, but the desire will bring about the proper results. The feeling of effortlessness is what is important.

--Jane Roberts/Seth

The will to win, the desire to proceed, the urge to reach your full potential. These are the keys that will unlock the door to personal excellence.

--Confucius

A creative man is motivated by the desire to achieve, not by the desire to beat others.

--Ayn Rand

Desire is the key to motivation, but it's determination and commitment to an unrelenting pursuit of your goal – a commitment to excellence – that will enable you to attain the success you seek.

--Mario Andretti

Human behavior flows from three main sources: desire, emotion and knowledge.

    --Plato

APRIL

The month of Inspiration

Inspiration is the process of being mentally stimulated to do or feel something, or to do something creative. Inspiration will occur when you read, think or hear something that gives you enthusiasm or a great desire to include a particular idea into your life. Inspiration will cause you to instantly understand the benefits to you of using a great idea.

Inspiration will give you the motivation to be all you can be, to be creative, to reach your goals, to learn from each other and to develop a feeling of enhanced well-being.

You can also develop your own inspiration when you spend some time allowing your thoughts to flow without limitations. For example, I like to jot down on my cell phone, any idea or goal I want to achieve when it unexpectedly pops into my mind. At that moment, I never think about the challenges it presents or worry about the how I may achieve it. Then, at a later time after I have given my subconscious time to develop these ideas, I can refocus on them and see what ways to achieve them pops into my mind. These new ideas can then become inspirational when I get a strong feeling of enthusiasm about them.

Things that inspire you may include some of these texts, doing new things, great accomplishments by those in sports, business and life, adventure, or whatever gives you a wonderful feeling about yourself.

Inspiration can work for you in many ways; it can awaken you to new possibilities when it lifts you above your ordinary experiences and limitations. It can get you out of a feeling of depression or apathy into a desire to find new possibilities and it can get you thoroughly engaged in a greater use of your own capabilities.

You can also have a goal to be an inspiration to anyone who crosses your path. You will find that they will reflect that inspiration back to you and magnify that inspirational feeling for both of you.

This next month, try to find some of the many ways that help you to become an inspiration to yourself and to those who cross your path.

Quotes on inspiration:

The most important thing is to try to inspire people so that they can be great in whatever they want to do.
   --Kobe Bryant

A good teacher can inspire hope, ignite the imagination, and instill a love of learning.
   --Brad Henry

Choose to focus your time, energy and conversation around people who inspire you, support you and help you to grow you into your happiest, strongest, wisest self.
   --Karen Salmanshon

To succeed, you need to find something to hold on to, something to motivate you, something to inspire you.

--Tony Dorsett

Our chief want is someone who will inspire us to be what we know we could be.

--Ralph Waldo Emerson

Concern yourself more with accepting responsibility than with assigning blame. Let the possibilities inspire you more than the obstacles discourage you.

--Ralph Marston

Don't be scared to fly high, 'cause it will inspire others.

--Kerli

MAY

The Month of Attitudes

Our attitude will be reflected in the position we take on any subject. We can also have a negative or positive bias toward how we see our world. Some people say our attitude is the filter through which we view our world.

If we pay attention to the few words that come out of a person's mouth about a subject, we can determine if their attitude about the subject is negatively or positively biased. The first words that come out of a person with a negative attitude will be about how something is bad. People with positive attitudes will have positive first words and have more natural energy. They generally will be more successful, more happy and more fun to be around.

It is easy to see from the above that attitude is the "little" thing that makes a big difference in our relationship and understanding of others.

Our attitude is what influences all our actions. It must be the right positive attitude if we are to expect positive results.

It is best to assume the best in others and spread optimism as you converse with them. Most people have 95% excellent qualities and 5% not so good qualities. When our attitude assumes and focuses on the best, then the best will be reflected back to us in our discussions and relationships with them.

Attitude can sometimes be determined by a person's body position, their facial expressions and their eye contact. If you see a person slouched in a chair, with the corners of their mouth pointing down (the Prussian smile) and unable to have eye contact with you, then it should be best to end the conversation and move out of their presence if possible. If the opposite is true, you will feel their energy presence and expect a great encounter.

It is also important to have a positive attitude about yourself and your abilities. Never depreciate yourself with negative phrases like "I am not good at something" or "I can't", because you will draw into your experience things that confirm those negative attitudes about yourself.

Quotes on Attitude:

Weakness of attitude becomes weakness of character.
  --Albert Einstein

Our attitude towards life determines life's attitude toward us.
  --John Mitchell

Two things define you: Your patience when you have nothing and your attitude when you have everything.
  --George Bernard Shaw

When a happy person comes into the room, it is as if another candle has been lit.
  --Ralph Waldo Emerson

Take the attitude of a student, never be too big to ask questions, never know too much to learn something new.
    --Maya Angelou

You can often change your circumstances by changing your attitude.
    --Eleanor Roosevelt

Attitude and enthusiasm play a big part in my life. I get excited about the things that inspire me. I also believe in laughing and having a good time.
    --Dwayne Johnson

Be positive. Your mind is more powerful than you think. What is down in the well comes up in the bucket. Fill yourself with positive things.
    --Tony Dungy

You must expect great things of yourself before you can do them.
    --Michael Jordan

JUNE

The Month of Knowledge

Knowledge cannot be given; it must be experienced. Knowledge is facts or information and skills obtained through learning experiences.

Today, there is so much information available on the internet and social media that it is difficult for us to determine what is fact and what is fiction. The only thing we can rely on is our experience and how this information can work to our future benefit. You must dig into some of the situations you are experiencing to determine whether you have enough information to thoroughly experience them. Simplicity should be of more value to you than complexity in experiencing anything.

If you really want to experience something, just start focusing your energy on it. Through the law of attraction, you will attract, from many sources, the information you need to fully experience your situation. When an experience works for you, it will have future value, and then it will naturally become part of your inner knowledge.

One test of the value of any experience is whether the experience is something that you can start using right away and continue to use it for your benefit in the future.

Consider the example about teaching or telling you that you can burn your finger on a hot stove. That information will probably fade away over a long period. However, once you experience burning your finger on a hot stove, the knowledge will never fade away because it has become part of your experience that resides in your eternal subconscious mind and does not reside in your physical brain like learning does.

Direct knowledge is knowledge arrived at through directly perceiving something in the moment. Some "aha" experiences could be considered direct knowledge provided that the knowledge is something you can continue to use for your benefit.

You may also experience something in a dream, from a trance channeler or by attuning with another entity, where the information you obtain can be experienced as a self-evident truth. If this experience is something that you can continue to use for your benefit, then it will have become part of your eternal inner knowledge.

This next month, try to distinguish the difference between learning and experiencing. You will then see that many of the things you are taught will just fade away over time and things that you experience will add to your eternal knowledge.

Quotes on knowledge and experience:

To know that we know what we know and to know that we do not know what we do not know, that is true knowledge.
　--Nicholas Copernicus

Opinion is the medium between knowledge and ignorance.
　--Plato

We are drowning in information but starved for knowledge.
　--John Naisbitt

The only real security that a man will have in this world is a reserve of knowledge, experience and ability.

--Henry Ford

A good decision is based on knowledge and not on numbers.

--Plato

No man's knowledge here can go beyond his experience.

--John Locke

JULY

The Month of Spontaneity

Spontaneity is simply the quality or state of being spontaneous or doing something without thinking it through beforehand.

With a little practice, you will be able to distinguish between which spontaneous actions come from our inner self and are helpful and enjoyable and those that are merely emotional reactions that may get you into trouble.

Our civilization is dependent upon the spontaneity and fulfillment of the individual. Our institutions have downgraded or denied spontaneity and focused on maintaining the status quo. This doesn't mean that we can't use and enjoy the wonderful application of spontaneity in our lives.

Your inner self does not emphasize seriousness in your life but is always spontaneously making available energy and direction to make your life more fun and fulfilling. Recognizing and acting on this spontaneity, which includes the joy that comes from your inner being, is something you can do to make your life more interesting and exciting. When you express yourself without holding back, you are automatically being spontaneous.

Your inner self keeps your heart, organs and cells operating spontaneously or you couldn't exist. Spontaneity will keep our outer life naturally going the same best way if we do not overthink it. All we need to do is to become aware of this spontaneity and to proceed with the exciting information it presents to us. This is why it is important to recognize that your first spontaneous thought is from your inner self. Once that first thought is subject to intellectual scrutiny, it loses its connection with your inner self and has little value to you.

This month try to spontaneously recognize your first thoughts by following through with them. Then you will discover the exhilaration that comes with those spontaneous experiences

Quotes on spontaneity:

Never say never. The things that you don't plan are the best. I'm a very spontaneous person.
   Lindsay Lohan

he very fact that it might not work is precisely why you should and must do this.
   Seth

Real laughter is spontaneous. Like water from the spring, it bubbles forth a creation of mingled action and spontaneity - two magic potions in themselves - the very essence of laughter - the unrestrained emotion within us!
   Douglas Fairbanks

Once we believe in ourselves, we can risk curiosity, wonder, spontaneous delight, or any experience that reveals the human spirit.

E. E. Cummings

Poetry is the spontaneous overflow of powerful feelings: it takes its origin from emotion recollected in tranquility.

William Wordsworth

Genuine happiness comes from within, and often it comes in spontaneous feelings of joy.

Andrew Weil

AUGUST

The Month of Thought Energy

We all hold energy in the form of thoughts, beliefs and emotions. In our three-dimensional (3D) reality we are learning about thought energy and how to use it to create what we want.

We participate in this 3D physical reality so that we can experience how creative our thoughts really are. While here, we can develop our abilities, learn and have learning experiences, create, solve problems and help others.

Knowledge about thought energy is learned when we discover through experience that thoughts and emotions can create our physical reality.

The first step is to notice that what you spend your time thinking about will eventually appear in your personal reality, when it is intently focused upon. This will also give you an idea of your inner development because your dreams, thoughts, expectations, beliefs and emotions will be literally transformed into your physical experiences.

What seems to be your perception of a concrete independent reality, is instead the materialization of your own emotions, energy and thoughts. Events in your life are actually focal points where highly charged thought impulses are transformed into something that can be physically perceived and experienced.

The most important task of your conscious mind is to focus your thoughts on the things you want and to shut out any thoughts of fear or worry or why you might not get it.

The intensity of a thought or image largely determines the immediacy of the physical materialization. Images or thoughts that are not completely materialized in your personal world could be a result of their intensity being too weak.

Focusing your thoughts on worry, negative relationships and fear will provide the thought energy for them to be created or reinforced in your life experience. Focusing on success and positive affirmations will make your life more successful, fun and exciting.

This next week, spend some time noticing where you are focusing your thoughts. Then see if some of those thoughts are translated into physical experience, whether good or bad.

Quotes on thoughts:

The greatest weapon against stress is our ability to choose one thought over another.
  --William James

You are given the gift of the gods; you create your reality according to your beliefs; yours is the creative energy that makes your world; there are no limitations to the self except those you believe in.
  --Seth

Poetry is when an emotion has found its thought and the thought has found words.

--Robert Frost

People demand freedom of speech as a compensation for the freedom of thought which they seldom use.

--Soren Kiekergaard

Desire is action. In the inner world, your desires bring about their own fulfillment, effortlessly. That inner world, and the exterior one, intersect and interweave. They only appear separate. In the physical world, time may have to elapse, or whatever. Conditions may have to change, or whatever, but the desire will bring about the proper results. The feeling of effortlessness is what is important.

--Seth

Learning without thought is labor lost; thought without learning is perilous.

--Confucius

Knowing what to do is very, very different from actually doing it.

--Seth

SEPTEMBER

The Month of Simplicity

Simplicity is the quality or condition of being easy to understand or do.

One of the most important benefits of simplicity is that it gives us a way to choose how we spend our time, money and energy. Simplicity will help us to recognize what is truly important by choosing among the many things that could take our time and effort. We can then eliminate those friends, activities or things that complicate our lives and take our time with little benefit to us. We can then simply focus on what is the best for us individually.

If a plan is simple, it focuses attention on just the important parts. The simplest stock trading plans and investment plans always work the best.

Simply put, simplicity makes things easy. This includes creative work, number and type of friends, social life, work habits, study habits, or any activity that consumes our time.

Brainy Quotes on the benefits of simplicity:

- Allows you to self-reflect.

- Reduces decision fatigue.

- Gives you a chance to engage in self-care.

- Fewer misplaced items.

- Removes friction from your life.

- Strengthens relationships.

- Increases focus.

- Encourages a clean and organized workspace.

Since we live in a society that thinks complex computer analysis creates better answers, it sometimes takes a little extra effort to jump on the simplicity train. Simplicity is staying in the present where everything happens, and simple solutions are more readily available.

Occam's Razor tells us that simpler explanations of observations should be preferred to more complex ones because they are more likely to be correct. His advice has survived the test of time.

Quotes on simplicity:

One of my mantras is focus and simplicity. Simple can be harder than you think. You have to work hard to get your thinking clean to make it simple. But it is worth it in the end, because once you get there, you can move mountains.
--Steve Jobs

There is no greatness where there no simplicity, goodness and truth.
--Leo Tolstoy

In character, in manner, in style, in all things, the supreme excellence is simplicity.
   --Henry Wadsworth Longfellow

I have just three things to teach: simplicity, patience and passion. These three are your greatest treasures.
   --Lao Tzu

Truth is ever to be found in simplicity, and not in the multiplicity of things.
   --Isaac Newton

OCTOBER

The Essence of Optimism

An optimistic person sees positive good things everywhere and is confident of the future. An optimist sees the world as full of opportunities and adventure. A pessimist lives in a dark negative world and sees the negative aspects of everything around him.

An optimist anticipates the best possible outcome of any endeavor and is willing to move on to expecting a different outcome, if a better one emerges.

Optimists believe in the power of positive thinking. They are always happy and see the glass as half full. Pessimists always see the glass as half empty.

In our society you will find people thinking they must choose between being optimistic, pessimistic or realistic. To me, realism means to be realistic about the probability of achieving the goals you select.

Many people hide behind the idea of realism when they cannot attain their goals by saying their goals were not realistic. People who rarely achieve their goals have given up too soon or they think any obstacle makes the goal too difficult for them to attain. If these people understood the power of desire, thoughts, beliefs and expectations, they wouldn't even consider thinking of obstacles, only success.

The only real obstacle you have that prevents you from reaching your goals is when you create a negative attitude and a negative focus. When the focus is on why you can't, then you can't. There is nothing you cannot achieve when you have optimistic positive thoughts, beliefs and expectations.

I make it a point to include, in my beliefs, the idea that you are never too old to set another goal or to dream a new dream. Goals and dreams can even be carried over into future lives if we run out of time to experience their attainment.

This month let's keep experiencing the power of optimism in those things we say and do.

Quotes on optimism/pessimism:

Optimism doesn't mean that you are blind to the reality of the situation. It means that you remain motivated to seek a solution to whatever problems arise.
— The Dalai Lama

I am essentially optimistic. Being alive is incredible. Life is extraordinary and beautiful. It can be hard and sad and terrifying, but it's all we've got.
— James Frey

Cynicism masquerades as wisdom, but it is the farthest thing from it. Because cynics don't learn anything. Because cynicism is a self-imposed blindness, a rejection of the world because we are afraid it will hurt us or disappoint us.
--Stephen Colbert

The optimist sees the rose and not its thorns; the pessimist stares at the thorns, oblivious to the rose.
--Khalil Gibran

A pessimist is one who makes difficulties of his opportunities, and an optimist is one who makes opportunities of his difficulties.
--Harry S. Truman

I always like to look on the optimistic side of life.
--Walt Disney

There are only two ways to live your life. One is as though nothing is a miracle. The other is as though everything is a miracle.
--Albert Einstein

Our greatest weakness lies in giving up. The most certain way to succeed is always to try just one more time.
-- Thomas A. Edison

NOVEMBER

The Month of Subliminal Messages

Subliminal messages are any sensory stimuli below an individual's threshold for conscious perception. This subliminal or hidden messages can activate specific regions of your brain without your conscious awareness and can cause you to do specific things such a buying a product, joining a group, or performing some action.

A subliminal or hidden message that is below your normal conscious limits of hearing or seeing, has the objective to control what you do. These messages are inaudible and invisible to your conscious mind but audible and visible to your unconscious, or subconscious mind.

You can receive subliminal messages when you are awake as the hidden part of a message that you see or hear. When you are asleep, you can also receive messages because your subconscious never sleeps. Your subconscious mind will faithfully carry out any instructions it receives, even if your conscious mind is not aware of it.

When my children first fell asleep at night, I sometimes whispered repetitive positive affirmations to them such as "there is nothing you cannot accomplish if you believe and expect that you can". Hopefully this helped them to accomplish what they wanted in their lives.

Commercial retailers have the practice of using subliminal words or images (stimuli) in their advertising that consumers won't consciously detect. This often involves words being flashed on a screen so briefly, less than one tenth of a second, that their conscious minds cannot register their appearance.

Subliminal messaging in advertising was first introduced as a concept by James Vickery and later reiterated by Vance Packard in his 1952 book The Hidden Persuaders and is today used by most advertisers and groups that want to control what you do.

What makes subliminal messages so unique is that they are below the threshold at which our conscious mind can perceive them. Since most meaningful decisions are made at the subconscious level, subliminal advertising will impact people's behavior and decisions to buy their products.

Subliminal messages can be used in a social media campaign to delight your viewers with something funny or crazy. Done well, this could lead to your ads going viral as people love sharing interesting social media posts.

Subliminal messaging can also include using the right colors to elicit the response to a message.

Below is the generally accepted meaning behind common colors and the emotions they evoke:

- Red: energy, action, physical needs (like hunger or affection), danger (the need for safety), excitement, strength.

- Orange: warmth, friendliness, hunger, fun, freedom, comfort.

- Yellow: cheerfulness, fun, vitality, happiness, optimism.

- Green: life, rest, wealth, freshness, health, peace, relaxation.

- Blue: trust, reliability, calmness, dependability, stability.

- Purple: spirituality, pride, luxury, sophistication, courage, mystery.

- Pink: sensitivity, romance, empathy, care, hope.

This next month, try to become aware of the many ways others try to set you up with subliminal messages in what you see and hear to get the action they want from you. When you feel an impulse to react a certain way to what you see or hear, don't react right away but wait and ask yourself: "what is the long-term benefit to me if I react to that impulse?" Just by thinking and mental questioning, you can get an idea of whether your reaction will benefit you or someone else. When you take the initiative to examine your real thoughts and are not afraid to react differently from the herd, you will find yourself in better control of your destiny.

Quotes on Subliminal Messages:

Control your own destiny or someone else will.
--Jack Welsh

You have absolute control over but one thing, and that is your thoughts.
--Napoleon Hill

Samurai I warrior - Mind your mind; guard it resolutely. Since it is the mind that confuses the mind, don't let your mind give in to your mind.

--Kaibara Tosani (1630-1714)

I saw a subliminal advertising executive, but only for a split second.

--Steven Wright

For warriors, if you calm your own mind and discern the inner minds of others, that may be called the foremost art of war.

--Suzuki Shosan (1579-1655)

Anything that causes you to overreact or underreact can control you, and often does.

--Paul Johnson

DECEMBER

The Month of Herd Instinct

The herd instinct, sometimes called herd behavior, is where people join in groups and follow the actions of others under the assumption that others know more than they do. This includes social, political, religious or any special group that has common beliefs about a subject. The herd instinct can cause things like riots, strikes and demonstrations when a herd forms a collective herd consciousness and a position against a power or principle.

This herd consciousness can have either a positive or a negative impact on us if we become a part of it. The positive impacts are when the herd accomplishes great things that we could never have done individually. You see this in sports and business teams along with man and animal groups that hunt together, worship together, fish together and work together.

The negative herd consciousness cans be found in riots, drunken brawls, gangs and old-time lynching groups. The herd instinct sometimes produces aggression toward those who are not members of their herd. When people can finally break away from the influence of a negative herd, they sometimes cannot believe some of the terrible things they did.

Investors can also be influenced by the herd instinct when they gravitate toward the most popular investments. The herd instinct of the investor can be seen on a large scale when they create asset bubbles with panic buying and market crashes with panic selling.

When herding occurs in stocks and other investments, including real estate, then investors will follow the emotion of the herd, instead of thinking for themselves as to whether the investment has merit for them.

Investors can avoid herding by having their own investing plan, thinking for themselves and following their own inner guidance. Investors need to become more aware of how their thoughts and beliefs can be influenced by the herd consciousness.

The important thing for us to remember about the herd instinct is that the herd consciousness can exert a tremendous pull on us to join in with them. Then once we become part of a herd consciousness, the experience can be either positive or negative.

We can get great enjoyment out of being a part of a herd consciousness in events like athletic games, parties, concerts, and group successes. If we can look for and become aware of the herd pull into a negative event, we can physically get away from the event and it will never negatively impact us.

This month, see if you can start recognizing the pull of the herd instinct. Then you can avoid the negative herds and enjoy the exhilaration of being part of a positive herd.

Quotes on herd instinct:

Once the herd starts moving in one direction, it's very hard to turn it, even slightly.
--Dan Rather

The herd instinct among forecasters makes sheep look like independent thinkers.
  --Edhar Fiedler

I don't live by a lot of society's rules; I can't pattern myself after the herd.
  --Kim Bisinger

I love my kids as individuals, not as a herd, and I do have a herd of children: I have seven kids.
  --Steven Spielberg

Collective fear stimulates herd instinct and tends to produce ferocity toward those who are not regarded as members of the herd.
  --Bertrand Russel

We herd sheep, we drive cattle, we lead people. Lead me, follow me, or get out of my way.
  --George Patton

Whenever you find yourself on the side of the majority, it is time to pause and reflect.
  --Mark Twain

THE 13TH MONTH

The Month of Inspiration for Investors

Money and the Goose, The Rule of 72, the Law of Compounding and The 6-1/2 % Rule.

Money and the Goose

Money can sometimes be analogous to owning a goose. There are three things you can do with your goose. You can eat the goose. You can keep the goose and eat the eggs, or you can keep the goose and keep some of the eggs to create more geese and eggs.

If you eat the goose or spend the money, in either case, you no longer have it. Second, you can keep the goose and eat the eggs, or you can spend the money you make. Third, you can keep the goose and keep the eggs to produce new geese.

Through the law of compounding, you can reach a point where you could not possibly eat all the new geese and eggs the geese produce. Now you have the goose that lays the golden egg. You can invest the money your goose money makes, until it makes so much money that you could never wisely spend it. Then you will become wealthy by having all the money you need and there will still be money compounding faster than you can spend it. This money will be available to be put to work for you. Your extra money will be your goose that lays the golden egg as it will infinitely continue multiplying by the law of compounding.

Your major task now is to put that extra money to work. You will discover that it is much easier to make money with money if you have a use for it and if that investment will also provide opportunities and jobs for others.

This next month, think of an opportunity that you would like to invest in that can respond to the law of compounding. Then think of a goal of a certain amount of money you might need to get started. Next start saving for that opportunity. Remember there is magic in thinking big. Then imagine that you have already obtained that opportunity. The more you focus your thoughts on that opportunity, with the expectation and belief that your subconscious will set up the best path to attain it, the quicker you will get it. If you believe that this creative system won't work for you, it won't. Always keep your thoughts positive and focused on what you want because they have tremendous power to create whatever you think about, whether good or bad.

Quotes on Money:

The lack of money is the root of all evil.
  --Mark Twain

When I was young, I thought money was the most important thing in life; Now that I am old, I know it is,
  --Oscar Wilde

An investment in knowledge pays the best interest.
  --Benjamin Franklin

The 13th month

I will tell you the secret of getting rich on Wall Street. You try to be greedy when others are fearful. And you try to be fearful when others are greedy.

--Warren Buffet

Money is only a tool. It will take you wherever you wish, but it will not replace you as the driver.

--Ayn Rand

Happiness is not the mere possession of money; it lies in the joy of achievement, in the thrill of effort.

--Franklin Delano Roosevelt.

Rule of 72 and The Law of Compounding

It is important that you get money working for you as early in your life as possible. This is because you will have both time and the magnificent Law of Compounding to work for you.

Considering Albert Einstein's compounding Rule of 72, when you divide your money return into 72, it will tell you how many years it will take to double your money. At six and a half percent compounded return, you would double your money every eleven years. At twelve percent return, you would double your money every six years.

The Rule of 72 will also tell you how many years it will take you to pay for something twice. At an interest rate of six percent, you pay for something twice every twelve years. Most people pay for their houses two to three times before they own it. It is important that we pay off debt as soon as we can because interest paid out is a wealth destroyer while interest reinvested is a wealth builder.

The Law of Compounding is one of the most important laws you will ever use if you want to become wealthy. That is why I have talked about it so much throughout my lifetime. The earlier in your life you start using the Law of Compounding, the more time you will have to have money working for you that compounds and the wealthier you will become. That is why the amount of money you work for is limited and is not as important as the money that works for you because it has no limit to the wealth it can create.

Quotes on compounding:

Enjoy the magic of compounding returns. Even modest investments made in one's early twenties are likely to grow to staggering amounts over the course of an investment lifetime.
--John Bogle

The compounding effect is the principal of reaping huge rewards from a series of small, smart choices.
--Daren Hardy

There will be good years and there will be bad years, but the compounding will continue unabated.
--Bryant McGill

Compounding has a snowball effect, it is just a tiny ball of snow at the very start, but it can turn into an avalanche over time.
--Naved Abdali

The strongest force in the universe is compound interest.
  --Albert Einstein

Time is your friend; impulse is your enemy. Take advantage of compound interest and don't be captivated by the siren song market.
  --Warren Buffett

The 6-1/2% Rule

There is investing magic in the six- and one-half percent rule. As far as I can find records, all assets have returned around an average of six- and one-half percent income plus appreciation over the very long term. This includes stocks, commodities, real estate, bonds, farmland etc. The important thing I saw was that the different types of assets do not all move at the same time. This gives us the opportunity to move some of our money around and into an asset that is beginning to move above the six- and one-half percent average. Our goal then is to more than double our money in eleven years (72/6.5).

All assets get overvalued when they move up faster than six- and one-half percent and then converge back to the six- and one-half percent mean. The long-term cycle for stocks and hard assets to get overvalued is 10-20 years. It can then take another 10-20 years of below average returns until the mean catches up to the price and the cycle starts all over again.

Because of the herd instinct, people are more apt to want to buy stocks and tangible assets when they are overextended above the mean or overvalued. The herd is then more apt to lose money when they sell the stock or tangible asset a few years later while the asset or stock is pulling back to the mean. This pullback to the mean is precisely where we want to buy stocks and assets.

When the herd goes crazy over an asset, begin looking for a trend change to sell it. When the herd is not interested in a stock or hard asset, look for a place to buy it. Assets like farmland and real estate that are difficult to buy and sell should not be traded but held and accumulated for the long term so that the Law of Compounding will work.

Trends go much further up or down than most people realize. An uptrend is when an asset price has price swings or zigzags that have higher swing highs and lows. A down trend is the opposite. A trend change is when the process reverses. Most prices and money-related activities establish a recognizable trend. Even professional gamblers chart blackjack tables for trends. They will jump into a game to bet against the dealer when the dealer is having a series of losses. The herd will usually do the opposite.

Stocks generally move up when commodities are consolidating or pulling back to the mean and vice versa. During inflationary periods commodities get overvalued while stocks pull back to the six- and one-half percent mean. In deflationary periods stocks will usually give better returns.

The important point to remember is that you should consider the price location of your investment relative to the long term six- and one-half percent mean before you buy or sell it. On assets that are easy to buy and sell, you may be able to double your returns if you take profits during the reversion to the mean rather than staying in that asset class for the very long term.

Quotes on Reversion to the Mean:

Reversion to the mean is the iron clad rule of financial markets.
--John Bogel

Historically, we have always seen reversion to the mean. After stocks have had an unusually great 10-20 years, they typically turn in subpar results the next 10-20. The next 10-20 years tend to be above average.

  --James O'Shaughnessy

More often than not, extreme events revert to the mean.

  --Coreen T. Sol

ABOUT THE AUTHOR

Paul William Johnson is a professional engineer, an entrepreneur and a former group vice president for a major construction firm in the Midwest. His groups included engineering, utilities, electrical, marketing and outside partnerships. He was also president of a major construction firm in the southwestern United States. Paul has also owned and operated his own engineering and construction firms.

Paul has served as an elected city councilman, a wastewater commissioner and a public works commissioner.

Paul has spent a lifetime of participation in choral and instrumental musical groups. He has crafted renaissance musical instruments and directed an early music group for ten years that performed for preludes and offertories in a large Presbyterian church in Southern California.

Paul has been a stock trader since 1960 and a commodity trader since 1970. Paul also participates in farming and owns farmland in Texas.

Paul managed the value engineering and cost reduction programs for the Metropolitan Water District of Southern California and was the Senior Owner Representative on the largest roller compacted concrete dam in California for the San Diego County Water Authority.

Paul is a writer and has published professional articles and papers along with several books that include <u>Creative Blogging for Personal or Business Improvement, how you do dat?</u> This book was entered in the Writers Guild contest and won first place in its genre. A second publication is titled <u>Thoughtful Texts to my Fantastic Grandkids</u>.

Paul has been married to his wife, Linda, since 1963. They have five children: four are engineers, entrepreneurs, farmers and investors and one is a university professor and a writer. All five children actively use the ideas and creative techniques described in this book.

Paul and Linda Johnson have thirteen wonderful grandchildren that have participated in writing the book, Thoughtful Texts to my Fantastic Grandkids.

There is great inner peace that comes when you discover that you can create whatever you want in your business or personal life.